TWO OR NINETY-TWO

For Youngsters and Oldsters
and Those Who Care for Them

ANNA MOW

June 18, 2002

To Dear Nell Anderson . . .

Given on the occasion of your 90th birthday. We cellbrate God's unique, steadfast creation in you! We give thanks for your place in Faith Church over so many years. May God continue to bless + guide + keep you, Nell, all the days of your life!

Brethren Press

With love + faith . . .
peace to you,
Pastor Erin Matteson for all of
Faith Church of the Brethren

This edition published in 2001 by Brethren Press, a program of
Church of the Brethren General Board, 1451 Dundee Avenue, Elgin, Illinois,
by special arrangement with Plough Publishing House.

05 04 03 02 01   5 4 3 2 1

Library of Congress Control Number: 2001098227

Manufactured in the United States of America

TABLE OF CONTENTS

INTRODUCTION 7

TO THE READER 9

PART I   VICTIMS OF KINDNESS

Victims of Kindness 12
Have Trust 15
In God's Hands 17
Why? I Don't Know 18
But God Knows 19
Suffering Is Expensive 20
No One Is Useless 21
Turn Concern into Prayer 22
Am I a Nuisance? 23
I Have the Lord 24
I Feel So Inadequate 25
Lonely? 26
Self-Centeredness Is Dangerous 26
Second Childhood? 27
It Is Not How You Feel 28
Be Ready to Change 28
Face Your Future 29
        To the Oldsters 31
        To Those Who Care for Oldsters 34

PART II   BOUNDARIES AND FREEDOM

New Babies Are Welcome 38
"Just His" Times 39
The Kindergarten, the Family 40
Good Music 42
Artwork – Outreach 43
Solitude and Silence 44
Learning to Wait 45

Choices 46
Negatives 46
When He Says No 47
Boundaries 48
Imagination 49
What About Spanking 49
Pets and Things 50
"Things" Are Not a Substitute 50
Relationships 51
Listening. 52
Get By with It? 53
Following 54
Responding to Love 55
Forgiving 56
Building Courage 56
God Love 57
        To the Youngsters. 59
        To Those Who Care for Youngsters 63
Anna's Prayer 67

ABOUT THE AUTHOR 68
ACKNOWLEDGMENTS 72

INTRODUCTION

Two or Ninety-Two comes from the unique perspective of Anna Mow in her ninety-second year. Though failing in body, her spirit would not be hindered.

Known as "Sister Anna," she lived a full and active life as a missionary, professor, traveling lecturer, and author. With her deep, childlike faith and big-heartedness, she brought a special touch of joy, love, and insight to people all over the world. Anna's direct and simple way was enriched by humor and her exceptional chuckle.

In her last months, a crippling stroke confined her to bed and wheelchair, impaired her speech and writing capabilities, and made her dependent on help from others for all her daily needs. It was not easy to be so suddenly hindered after a very active life, but with determination and courage, she dictated this book to her family.

Some days Anna managed to sit at her desk in a wheelchair and dictate freely for "the book." Other times, those around her wrote down her spontaneous comments. There always had to be a notebook handy!

As she became weaker and less able to dictate, she

encouraged us to use "anything you want from books I've already written." Quotations from two of her books, *So Who's Afraid of Birthdays* and *Preparing Your Child to Love God,* have been woven into the thoughts and wisdom of her final months.

This is Anna Mow's last book, one she didn't live to see in completion. With an urgency — which intensified in her last weeks — she shared her struggles as an invalid, her joy in children, and her lifetime message of hope and praise to God. Her message was always clear and straightforward, pointing to love, service, and a God-centered life.

"Glory be!" she said. "It's the same message I've had all along."

———————

Reading over the notes our grandmother dictated to us, we marveled at how much she was able to convey in spite of her physical handicaps. We sensed again the urgency with which she wanted to proclaim her message.

We chuckled, remembering the twinkle in her eye and the finger wagging to emphasize "That's the point!" We could hear her contagious laugh and feel her firmly grounded faith as she praised God's greatness with a voice loud and clear. "I'm in God's hands!" she would declare. We felt challenged and privileged that we could experience Mother's last five months in our home.

We hope her witness can bring hope and courage to others who suffer and to those who care for the old or the young.

The Mow Family

To the Reader

I am writing for the ninety-year-olds and the two-year-olds. I am writing also for the ones halfway in between who take care of the ninety-year-olds and the two-year-olds.

What is the difference between being a helpless eighty- or ninety-year-old and being a helpless two-year-old? There is actually a similarity. We can learn from it without having disrespect for the eighty-year-old.

I'm ninety-one years old. I'm still a whole person even though I'm ninety-one.

But I've had a stroke.
I have to be taken care of.
It is a need to me.
Others must experience that same need.
I have a message for them —
    a message for those
    who go through what I do.
It's the same message I've had all along.
It's for the oldsters.
It's for the youngsters.
And it is for all those in between.

Yes, I had a stroke, and sometimes I get words mixed up. And I find there are some people who've never had a stroke and don't have a very good use of the language either. Ha! At least I have a good excuse.

My body is old. But I'm not.

Anna Mow
May 1985

9

PART I

The first time I thought of it, I laughed.
You'll be surprised.
My subject? — I'm ashamed to tell you —
but the title of this part is . . .

VICTIMS OF KINDNESS

FOR OLDSTERS
AND THOSE WHO CARE FOR THEM

VICTIMS OF KINDNESS

Everybody says to me, "Aren't you marvelous! I would like to be old. I'm looking forward to old age and the freedom of old age."

When you are very old
everybody does something for you.
You are always there waiting,
waiting for someone to do something.
When you want to do something,
they say, "No. You can't. You're not able."
You can't do this, you can't do that.
They say, "You aren't strong enough yet.
You aren't well enough yet."

I feel like a victim of kindness.
I can't fight that. I don't want to fight that.
Here I am.
I can't complain about anything.
But I'm caught in a corner.
Nobody knows how many times I feel cornered.
I don't think I'm the only one.
Every invalid must go through that.
We don't have the same kind of treatment
we were used to before.
I never had anybody tell me when to go to bed
and when to get up.
I'm just here — stuck and waiting.
I'm at the mercy of my family and my good friends.
I'm too old — now I'm no good.
How can I be of service?
I've been teaching for years;
now *I* am handicapped and *I* need help.
  I mean it when I cry out,
  "I need help."
Everybody needs help. I'm so helpless.
Keep really close touch with me so I've nothing to worry about.

HAVE TRUST

It's something to get to the place where you don't know your name or where you are. That's how far I got. Babies don't know their names. Babies just lie there and trust. I can do that. I can trust just like a baby.

I am ready to take anything God sends — not only what "God sends," but what "God lets happen." That's important.

There are certain things I can't do all right.
I am here in a world of suffering.

I can't even choose what kind of suffering I'll have. But I can choose what my attitude is going to be toward suffering.

No matter how great a person's suffering or loss, he is still free to decide how he will take his condition — whether he will yield to it or stand up to it. In the process he will find that he becomes more concerned about a meaning for life than a meaning for suffering. In finding a meaning for life, he can take whatever happens to him.

Even if there may be nothing to do for oneself or for others, one can still worship. Worship makes thanksgiving possible. Thanksgiving opens the heart for God and for being a blessing to every available person. It will bring an end to any feeling of uselessness. We must trust God to take everything and work it out to his glory.

In God's Hands

My son keeps saying to me, "You are in God's hands," or "It will come in God's time." Glory be! It's the same I've been telling people all along. Now I'm in it. Of course I know that. I have faced that. But I am writing this especially for people who are in the same situation.

Many Christians today who talk of the love of God say at the same time that disease and suffering come from him. They should read the prologue to Job. God *permitted* the tragedies to come. He did not bring them. Job was in his care all the time.

No matter what happens to us, we are within his loving care. Our Lord suffered. Paul's thorn in the flesh was never taken away. We may suffer. If we trust him, the suffering will never be useless. He is the Great Physician to the whole person. He always gives courage, hope, and faith.

We are in God's hands. Those are *good* hands!

WHY? I DON'T KNOW

One thing came to me since I had the stroke. It came through what people write to me. I have all kinds of letters. There are some who cannot understand why I had a stroke when I do the Lord's will. "Why should God let this happen to you?" they write.

But pain is part of the experience of being human. I am human. You are human. Jesus came into this crazy world and he suffered.

In all the things I've been through because of the stroke, I have found out something about healing. I believe in healing. I believe I have been healed several times. It was a wonderful thing when the doctor said I wouldn't live and then I was healed.

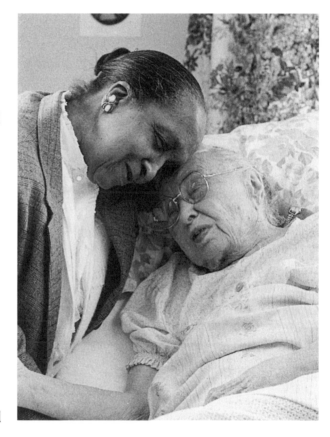

But now here I am, knocked out from a stroke, and I've told the Lord, "Here I am, waiting to be healed."

Now if I'm not healed — what next? That's what I've had to face. If anyone can give comfort to anyone in this situation, I say, God bless them.

But God Knows

Why am I not healed? I don't know. But God knows, and he'll take care of me. I don't know whether I'll be healed, but it doesn't matter. I have entered into a relationship with him — of accepting sickness and trouble.

We can say, "Lord, will you please heal me so I don't have to be weak?" We can say, "I *want* to be healed. I want *that*." But answers don't come because of what I *want* out of it.

I've come to the place where I realize that the thing wrong with the church is that we just want salvation — what you get out of this, what you get out of that.

If we were healed every time instantly, we could misuse the heavenly Father. If we are not healed, we wait for him. And we have the illustration of the cross. Jesus wanted help. God didn't give it to him, or there wouldn't have been the cross.

To the true follower of Jesus, healing is not an isolated experience for special occasions or needs. It is an experience for the whole of life and for the whole person. Jesus' work of healing the body was only one part of his healing ministry. He healed people from sin and all its scars. He healed them from broken relationships. He healed them to be made whole persons with a new capacity to love.

A relationship with God is the most important thing in life; it is more important that God lives than that we live.

Sometimes we've got the healing and sometimes we don't. *But we've got the same Lord!*

Suffering Is Expensive

God does not desire suffering as an end in itself, I am sure. But all suffering is so expensive He will not let it be wasted. He will use it for his children's growth.

The first purpose of our lives must be, "Thy kingdom come, thy will be done." This is never a passive statement of endurance or of mere agreement to submit to whatever happens. It is a positive statement of the will to reach out for that which will bring glory to God. I am also sure that the greatest prayer we can pray is, "Whatever brings the greatest glory to God, I want it, even if it brings suffering and loss to me."

No One Is Useless

What are we doing here for Jesus? He doesn't want us to be here for nothing. We can pray. Then we can see what else to do. In the meantime the love of the Lord can come down and work for us so we aren't crippled any more and we can know his presence. He's in our hearts — in our crippled hearts. It's the miracle of the whole story.

No one is ever useless to God. No one who can pray is ever useless.

There are many people to perform the needed activities, but too few to take the time for prayer.

I suppose the hardest thing about being an invalid, about being "useless," is that it is much harder to receive help than to give it. It is much harder to be still than to be active. This is why it is important to learn how to be a gracious receiver as well as a gracious giver.

I'm so thankful that God has the answer, *no matter what.*
And so we face the next day.

Turn Concern into Prayer

Prayer is a very special ministry open to invalids, a privilege and a responsibility. Turn every concern into a prayer. God's concern is always greater than ours. You can cooperate with him as you pray by helping him to answer your prayers, even if it is no more than a smile or a show of loving patience.

My mother was an invalid and spent her last seven years not only helpless in body, but speechless too, from several strokes. Her mind was clear, her heart was warm, one hand was still in good condition, and her

listening ears were in perfect working order. She was in our home in Chicago for three years, and she was a blessing to us all. Even some of my theological students would come to visit her and go away uplifted. She always smiled at the right time, and her one hand could reach out to express the sympathy or joy of her heart.

Am I a Nuisance?

One time I said, "I'm a nuisance." But my son Merrill said, "Mother, do you remember when I was a baby? Was I a nuisance?" I answered him, "Look here, young man. You be careful. There are many in the world who would have counted their child a nuisance, but I *never* did! Sometimes I didn't know what to do with you. I'll tell you, sometimes I really didn't. But I wouldn't have given you up for a minute."

And do you know what my son said? "So that's the way it is with you, Mother. You are never a nuisance."

God bless him.

I Have the Lord

I experienced the Lord's presence yesterday. Now my condition doesn't matter.

I have the Lord.
The emphasis in all this is as I never saw it before — to give *everything* over.

Yesterday I felt the Lord touched me. That's more than those paper angels in my mobile do. But they are a good illustration anyway.

The Lord came to me — I'd be scared if he hadn't. I don't need an angel with wings (like those in the mobile) to come to me when I know *he* is here.

I pray to the Lord, "Lord, do what you want. You can heal me or not. I don't mind as long as I can praise *you!*"

I'm *not* asking for healing or miracles. People today ask and pray for something to happen and it's just for themselves. God can heal me or not. It doesn't matter; I'm just here to do what he asks of me. I can praise *him*, no matter what.

Put everything in God's hands, and he will work in your life.

I Feel So Inadequate

I was so negative this morning.
I didn't want anybody to say anything to me.
Everything in me rebelled.
I need quiet,
not just to speak, but to listen.
Here I am in bed.
And I didn't want to be here.
I haven't finished facing it.
People do everything for me.
They are so kind.

We are going to give you a kindness," they say, "a shower," or "a walk." I'd rather wash myself. I don't want to use the walker — it gets in the way.

I'm told a hundred times a day, "This is good for you." I'm so tired of things that are good for me. That's no criticism. I have nothing to criticize. My goodness, they only do things that are good for me!

When I feel so inadequate, I need to call on God. It's like John wrote:

Truly, truly, I say to you, when you were young, you girded yourself and walked where you would; but when you are old, you will stretch out your hands, and another will gird you and carry you where you do not wish to go.

— John 21:18, RSV

25

LONELY?

Lonely? I've never been so lonely in my life! But—those who know the Lord are never alone. Solitary times are opportunities to know him in greater depth. In order to be free for this new level of being, all self-pity must be conquered. Anything that is of self-centeredness must be recognized as the enemy it is.

God cannot squeeze into a self-centered heart. His abundant grace awaits an open door. "Be still, and know that I am God (Ps. 46:10).

Being *alone* does not necessarily mean *loneliness*. Your condition depends more on how you get along with yourself than on how little you possess. If you have a great emptiness in your life, you are not only alone but lonely. If your security has depended on others, or on their dependence on you, then when left alone, you are lonely. Poverty of mind and soul is poverty indeed and loneliness indeed.

When you know the secret of life – Christ in you – you will never be left stranded, no matter what happens to you. Even though your body changes with the years and many activities cease, this inner life can become more real all the time. In the quietness of the hours when you are seemingly alone, you can know his thought for you in your every need.

SELF-CENTEREDNESS IS DANGEROUS

If you feel unwanted, unneeded, laid on the shelf, no good to anyone, unappreciated—watch out! All these feelings of being neglected are evidence of thinking from self-centeredness, and they are all dangerous.

Stop clinging to the wrong self and open your life to the true self, which is possible through Christ.

If this lesson was poorly learned when you were sixteen, it may be hard at sixty. It may not have shown up very much in your years of active service when you were considered a very unselfish person in your busyness. The test comes when the activity stops!

SECOND CHILDHOOD?

No one needs to be in a second childhood. There is nothing wrong with old age, unless you become self-centered.

I wonder how many older people act childish because it is expected of them, or because they find it easy to get away with? (Or maybe they never outgrew their first childhood!)

We are expected to give up our childish ways. God's picture of *true maturity* is in 1 Corinthians 13.

The Apostle Paul left no room for the Christian to revert to childish ways: "Love [which is maturity] knows no limit [even in years] to its endurance, no end to its trust, no fading of its hope; it can outlast anything" (1 Cor. 13:7, Phillips).

We keep on growing to the end of life.

It Is Not How You Feel, But How You Think

I do not believe for one minute that we are only as old as we *feel*. We do not always feel young, but we can — with sound minds — choose our actions.

Our bodies may wear out, our knees may stiffen, our joints may creak. But I do believe the Spirit-controlled child of God is only as old as he *thinks*.

Be Ready to Change

A person's whole life is really a preparation for aging. If you have an interest in a lot of things, and if you enjoy being alone at times, then aging isn't really difficult. If people do not learn how to live before they are sixty, they will be in trouble after sixty. Changes go with aging all through life. I think the key is adaptability. You must be ready to change to survive. Don't be afraid of change.

It has been said that old age begins the moment we lose the flexibility to change.

God never changes, but our minds must be open to new knowledge or they grow stagnant. When we quit growing, we begin to die.

It is never too late to begin all over again. Hope and a new beginning are always possible for anyone.

Be new territory for the Lord. Don't fight something new; don't get stuck in old ways. Don't be afraid of the "new." Don't defend the old. Don't imitate the gospel. Don't imitate the message or the form. Follow the Holy Spirit. Then you will get some place.

There are a lot of things to be learned yet. We have to keep on learning even if we are ninety-one.

FACE YOUR FUTURE

I'm not very good at thinking about the future. But am I ready for it? Facing your future is one of the hardest things. It all depends on your relationship to God and to other people.

Of course, there are those who, in all their lives, have never come into a living relationship with God, who have never prayed except in moments of despair. But no one is too old to discover him. So far as God is concerned, we never have any time but now. And he always comes in wherever he is let in.

A Christian prepares for his future by *living* every day of his life in a way to be pleasing to God. His preparation is not in an accumulation of material treasures stored away, but in a life of love and service lived in this world now.

The fact is, if I look at God as a loving God, then I have no fear of the future, neither the immediate future nor the long-term future.

For some people "being in the hand of God" means facing death. For me it does not mean that; it means God is going to help me this week.

I still have a choice: to trust in God or not.

TO THE OLDSTERS

What shall I say to the ninety-, or to the seventy-, or to the eighty-year-old who is going through what I go through? The pesky thing is that I can still think and talk, but I'm not able to write down what I want to. That's a need. (Everyone does everything for me.) I'd like to say a few things to the old folks who experience this and who go through what I go through.

- **Accept it**

  Accept it when others take responsibility; talk things over with them. Be glad for all the help. The older a person becomes, the greater blessing he should be to all those who are still in places of active responsibility; the more encouraging he should be to those who are younger.

- **Have patience**

  There are more things I'm learning now. They are more about patience than anything else — the value of patience. Accept what happens to you. You can become a creature of kindness when you can't do anything else.

- **Face it**

  Face the facts. Wait and be shown how. That is a challenge.

- **Be a listener**

  One of the greatest needs of the world today is for *listeners.* If you are incapacitated for any other service, this ministry is still open for you. If you are willing to be an ear for the Lord, people will come to you. They want to know about a Heavenly Father who can meet every need.

- **Never be bitter**

  The big obstacle to God's grace is bitterness. Some people complain because they are not blessed by God as others have been. They do not realize that in thinking of themselves, they open the door to bitterness and close it to God's grace. No matter what happens, we dare never be bitter or resentful.

- **Keep steady**

  If you can manage it, then do it. But there are "almosts" in life. When you are disturbed because you don't *quite* make it, keep steady. You think you will be able to "do this" or "do that," but there are a lot of things that are "almost." Jesus also meets this "almost" area.

- **Don't be afraid**

  Instead of being afraid, do the best you can under the circumstances. Guard against any anxiety about the future. Anxiety is the enemy of faith and is certainly its opposite.

  Eternal life does begin now. We have "today," and we live it in his presence and through strength given us by his Holy Spirit. So remember the shining secret: If we are not afraid for today, we need not be afraid for tomorrow.

- **Be thankful**

  Give thanks for God and his love, for a Redeemer, for the Holy Spirit. If you are suffering, thank God for doctors and nurses. If you are alone, be thankful that with him you are never really alone.

- **Wait**

  We must wait for the joy that is coming. We must wait *now*. Waiting is our faith. There won't be any room for those weepy things if we wait for the joy. We wait for the joy of the now.

- **Love**

  Love those who care for you. Love those around you. If you don't love people, you can't love God. If you don't love God, how can you understand how God loves people? In this day and age, we must find the love

  that changes our attitude toward other people.

  Even if you don't understand everything, if you *love* the people, you can help them. We never grow too old to love, and it is never too late to learn to love with a "giving love" (*agape*). No need to be bound by past loveless years. Any day can be a new beginning. It is this kind of love that turns eyes of faith and hope to the future and makes life worth living — at any age.

- **Do not lose courage**

  As long as there is hope there is life. It is life that counts.

  Whenever I think of my father, I think of life, or real zest for living. He never grew old, though he lived ninety-one years. He never lost courage, a courage made of endurance and hope.

  So many of us have no expectancy. I don't mean expecting aches, pains, and disabilities. That is devastating. Anyone who never loses courage or hope is free to look for the best in the future.

To Those Who Care for Oldsters

I want to say this to those who are with old people:

- **Reassure them**

    When they say, "Am I in the right place?" just reassure them. That's all they need. There's a request in it when they ask that. I asked that often. I wasn't sure where I was. "Am I in the right place?" You can just answer, "You are."

- **Be patient**

    Don't always say, "Relax." I've heard it more than a thousand times. Everyone says, "Relax." Even my beloved husband says it to me. He says, "Relax and take life easy." But you sometimes just can't relax – and that's a fact. Be patient with those who can't relax.

- **Have a good laugh**

    I could write a whole chapter for the "Victims of Kindness" about how and when to laugh. A good laugh is so important. Keep a sense of humor.

- **Don't blame them**

    Don't blame the old people for being over-anxious. People who you think would have no anxiety at all might still have it.

- **Take care**

  Hang up the pictures the children make for them. Take care of the greetings and cards they receive, and put the addresses in their book. Don't be a "victim of carelessness."

- **Comfort them**

  It's nice when someone comes and holds my hand. It is security. It's nice for someone ninety.

- **Let them choose**

  Choices are important to kids and are still something to older people. I'm glad when I can say, "I'd rather have cranberry juice." Everybody likes some freedom in this area.

- **Give extra**

  Something of an extra touch at mealtimes is appreciated. The special things like pineapple bits in the applesauce or a tasty sauce on the rice make the difference.

- **They should do what they can**

  In many places old people are taken advantage of. Old people face life and think they are old, but they carry life-giving strength. More than they know.

There are old people who *think* they are old and then don't do things for themselves. I say to them, "You behave yourself and do the things *you* can."

- **Let the children visit**

I love children. I may get tired, but I'm never too tired for babies. Keep the little ones close to the old ones. Not only is it natural, it is important. (Where I'm living with my son — with his family at the Bruderhof — there is a natural setup for this.)

The fact is that older people are usually grandparents. They have a natural contact with children. The children don't worry if we are old or not. That's the thing that moves me — a little one like one-year-old Eric just takes charge of me. He takes over my shoe and unties it. It can be kept natural.

I know oldsters who don't have grandchildren who find a way to be with children — in the church or working in a hospital. What contact do old people have with children? That's the question. *Keep the little ones with the old ones.*

PART II

*We want the children to be free
in this crazy world.
We could call this chapter . . .*

BOUNDARIES AND FREEDOM

FOR YOUNGSTERS
AND THOSE WHO CARE FOR THEM

*No child is so insecure as the one
who doesn't know his boundaries.*

New Babies are Welcome

*A new baby?
That means there's hope
from God.
We all welcome new
babies because every-
body loves them!*

When a new baby arrives, that is one time he can be the center of attention. Each baby is welcomed as an individual. Even if they come as individuals, a baby is part of a family right from the start. Each one has a story of his own: "He looks like his uncle," or "He has his daddy's nose." Oh, the joy and welcome when a new baby is introduced!

A baby's first smile is indeed a big event in his life — bigger than he knows! It means his capacity to respond is developing properly. The mother is smiling the child to smile back. When the infant responds to love, he is learning the first lesson in responding to God, for God is love. Love alone has this drawing power — to bring life development out of another in the best way possible.

I attended a welcome party this morning for three new babies. This was their first party. The joke was that the mothers traded babies before they came in to meet everybody. So when they came, we couldn't figure out which one was which. The little boy was in a pink blanket, and the little girl wore a blue cap. That was a good one!

"Just His" Times

There are many special times that come in a child's life that are "just his." First is when he is born! Then comes each birthday. There are many times that stand out for each child in his lifetime. These are important. They help the child develop to be his or her real self. Children need to learn to know themselves as individuals. They also need to know themselves as part of a group. They need to know themselves in relation to others.

But what happens when a child is in a group of children? Does he become "one of a crowd"? Does he have to toe the line and walk exactly the same way? Do the children learn to know themselves as individuals when they are in a group situation?

Nobody has to be afraid. A child can be part of a group, and it doesn't take anything away from the individual.

THE KINDERGARTEN, THE FAMILY

The child in kindergarten! The discipline that little children get hold of when they are with other children is important. Children experience in kindergarten a sense of "groupness," a learning to get along with others. Every person needs both togetherness and separateness in order to develop his best selfhood.

There is no question about the needs of a child for love and affection, for belonging, for acceptance, for understanding, for a sense of achievement, but the test to whether these emotional needs have been met in a Christian way comes when the child becomes an integral member of a group outside the home.

If these needs have been met in the home, as they should have been, the child will never have to lean on the group for security, nor will he have to yield to the group against his own inner convictions in order to have acceptance.

Before kindergarten, what do children learn in the family? Can that little boy get along with his brother and his sister? Does he know how to obey his parents? What does he learn in his family relationships — in getting along? Then, having learned at home, he's ready for the experience in kindergarten. He has to learn how to behave with consideration for other people, how to get along with other children. This is the background for later on — for the right relationship between boys and girls. Even in kindergarten the boys learn to be kind to girls, not to be rough, to be responsible.

Four- and five-year-olds are at an especially important age. In their studies educators see the importance of this age for a child's learning. Even in scientific books, they are saying that five-year-olds understand things about life that nobody else understands. And we don't even realize it!

The family unit prepares the child for his education. The family and kindergarten go together. That's absolutely true. Very true. I could write a whole chapter on that.

GOOD MUSIC

Whenever I see a child who responds to good music, I'm up on my toes right away. Children are natural. They love good music. They love it when there's rhythm; they respond to it. When do you start singing with a child? I say when they are born — and before.

A lot of folks never think about what good music does to the child. Get them prepared. What they hear at home will help them recognize good music.

I was in a home where silence is practiced at the beginning of each meal, followed by a song of thanksgiving. When I was in this home, the two-year-old broke the silence by saying joyously, "Sing Alleluia, sing Alleluia." Even for the smallest child, singing together in the family becomes a spontaneous expression of gratitude.

Artwork – Outreach

The child does all kinds of outreach. His artwork is a good example. I've especially saved the things my grandchildren have written and all of their artwork. Every child knows what to do with a crayon or a pen and pencil. It is wonderful.

One of the neglected spheres of training the imagination is in the field of art. Many children get no encouragement, because they are given only lines to stay inside of for coloring. Of course, these coloring books give muscle training and leeway for color choice, but they give no opportunity whatever for the language of a child's imagination.

Turn a child loose. See what he will do. Nobody should be pushing him and saying, "*Don't* do it this way. *Don't* spoil our program. *Don't* spoil our this. *Don't* spoil our that."

Some children did pictures for me when I was in the hospital. They were turned loose with the story of my being sick. They drew pictures. Some pictures were crazy, and some had a lot of sense. But nobody was telling them what to draw. They were told I was sick. They loved me. *Everything* was in those pictures — from a blue donkey to an angel.

Entering into the experience of another person is something children are good at, especially when they hear that someone is sick.

I'll tell you,
you'll have lots more
bright colors
if you turn children
loose.
You bet your boots!

Solitude and Silence

Sometimes children need quiet rather than a lot of talking to. Sometimes they just need to be left alone, to have some solitude — not put some place where they are afraid, but so that they have time to think. When my children were little, I taught them often about solitude.

If a mother yells at a noisy child to be quiet, he may be cowed into silence, but he won't learn anything about the value of silence. A whisper and a raised finger, "shhh," can be made into a game that brings a willing, joyful response. This is practice for the times when it is expected of him to be quiet. If she plays silence with him, he will find out a quietness of soul that is important to the child as well as his mother. He can "play silence" long before he can enjoy taking orders to be silent.

At any age it seems we can join with the little one who has discovered "this quiet is just what I wanted."

LEARNING TO WAIT

The wonderful thing about the May Pole today was that everybody — old and young — was there. Each grandma, each grandpa, each grandchild, each daddy and mommy was out.

Free, open play. I'd never seen this since I was a child. The freedom! That was wonderful. Each child watched which ribbon he wanted to follow.

Children...Cooperation and action...Play...Pageantry...Color...Freedom.

That is something! Traditions like these should not be lost.

The May Day celebration is a wonderful annual affair for a child. I'm glad it is not lost. All spring they get ready for it. They worked for weeks getting ready for this May Pole. The children began preparing and thinking ahead about the first of May. They learn to wait for this because it has a specific date. The whole game is freedom. There is freedom even with learning to wait for a certain time. *Learning to wait is important.* It is important for the child's future.

CHOICES

Now, little fellow, if you get everything you want in this world, would it be good for you? One little boy eats as much as he wants and keeps on. What happens?

If I give you everything you want, would you like that? Of course you would. But what about the tummy ache?

Any place where the parents can let the child make a choice, they should. It is very important. Any place you can turn children loose and let

them make a choice, do it!

Only the youth who has learned to choose, and has learned the discipline of the responsibility of maintaining a choice, will be free to choose God and his way.

Adults always need to remember that the responsibility of choice must eventually be transferred to the child. To have the child accept this moral responsibility is the goal of our training. Most conscientious parents recognize the importance of this transfer, but too often they fail to realize that the path to that goal is made up of *seemingly insignificant incidents* day by day.

NEGATIVES

The worst thing that comes to youngsters is that someone is always saying, "*Don't* do this. *Don't* do that." They are up against negatives all the time and are never free to experiment. We want them to be free in this crazy world. That includes telling children, "You be good. You do this." This is the hardest one for the parents. This bossiness. When a mother gets bossy, that's a curse! The use of authority is hard for us to learn.

The secret is to be a *servant!* Very few people have ever really learned how to use authority. When mothers get bossy and roar at their children, that is not the secret of the Christian life. Jesus said over and over again, "I called you to be servants!" When we are servants, we think, "What can I do that helps other people take their own responsibility?" When we learn that, we learn how to take care of children. If we know the secret of service as Christians, we are closer to the Lord than in any other way.

WHEN HE SAYS NO

The developing self in a child has to be able to say no before a genuine yes can be said. Wise parents will help him experiment with no's by helping him foster good interest he has in things outside himself.

As he becomes conscious that he is somebody who can speak for himself, he goes through a self-centered stage, which is healthy. (The only trouble is that too many never learn to go beyond this self-centeredness, which is a sign of growth at three, but a sign of death at forty.)

A three-year-old is just learning to know himself in relation to his little world. It is normal for him to

be self-centered because he has just discovered himself. But if his parents are wise, he will find out that even though he is dearly loved, he is still not the center of the universe. He will learn to make room for others who are also important.

BOUNDARIES

No child is so insecure as the one who never knows how far he can go. That is what I have said over and over again. It is one of the truest things I have ever experienced.

How do we know where to set the boundaries? *We* have to set the boundaries. *We* have to decide where a child has freedom but does not hurt

himself or someone else. If a child touches the stove, after he has been told not to, he soon discovers that he had better listen to his mother.

The parents have to set these boundaries, and the children have to learn that they can trust their parents.

Children have more concern about what is right or wrong than we think. But if a child doesn't know his limits, he never has freedom. That's one of the things that's been wrong.

If he doesn't know his boundaries, then he is so insecure he can do any bloomin' crazy thing he pleases.

IMAGINATION

Let their imagination develop. Trained imagination opens the door to the greatest adventures of life. A healthy imagination is called *faith*. When the imagination is undeveloped, retarded in any way, diseased, we call it worry or anxiety. In worry and anxiety, fear is in control rather than faith.

Imagination is the bridge to the understanding of others. When a child can imagine enough so that he can enter into the feeling of another person, it is an important day in his spiritual development. When he can say, "Mommy, are you tired? Let me help you," a new sense of fellowship is possible between mother and child.

Imagination is also the bridge into the future. Above all, our imagination needs to be trained so we can have real faith.

WHAT ABOUT SPANKING?

I say the question is not "What about spanking?" but "What do you do besides spanking?" You see, if parents don't love the children, spanking isn't worth *anything*.

God is *love*. It's only when kids know *God loves us* that they have security. I don't know a quicker way for anybody to find out about God-love than to know family-love.

Don't be afraid of discipline.

The fact that discipline and disciple come from the same root word is suggestive of the positive meaning of discipline. Anyone can punish a child, but only those who can make disciples of the children can truly discipline them. When we see discipline as a positive directive in life, we no longer do something *to* a child but we do something *for* him or *with* him so that he will want to change for the better.

If you don't discipline, the children won't know where the limits are. There's no child so insecure as the one who isn't disciplined properly.

Pets and Things

Pets are very good for children. The children will learn alot from pets. If they don't treat the cat right, it will scratch. This way they learn.

A child needs to learn to take care of things — his own pet, things that might break, things that belong to others.

When a child learns to know what is "mine," then he can have respect for what is "thine."

"Things" Are Not a Substitute

Jesus came to earth to reveal to us that the most important fact of true religion is that we can have relationship with him. Since God is love, this relationship must be one of love — giving love (*agape*) and not a mere receiving love.

It may be that part of our blindness to the value of giving love in the building up of relationships is that we get lost in the giving of things. Things can so easily become a substitute for love. Then the things become tools in a relationship and an indication of lack of love. But the children know when a gift is a substitute for love instead of a token of love. A child's security is never in things but in personal relationships.

RELATIONSHIPS

Parents, indeed, hold the key to the atmosphere of the home. If the peace of God in their hearts holds against all pressures from without, all frustrations, all differing opinions, and family emergencies, then their children will also learn to know this same peace. They will know that this peace cannot be broken by any outside influence.

The children will also experience a sense of security as the family relationships are strengthened by difficulties met together. This will help them know that their security is in these close relationships rather than in things. This stable security of the home relationship will bear fruit in healthy *courage* that cannot be broken by any untoward or cruel experience in the world outside the family.

LISTENING

How to listen to a child is part of learning. How do I listen? It is a common thing for children that they have nobody to listen to them. Listen. You can create fear in children if you don't listen. Don't scare and punish them. Rather listen. Mother is too busy and doesn't

listen but just gives orders and goes. How do you listen even to a baby? A mother soon knows a lot about her baby when she stops to listen.

Suppose a child falls and then kicks at the thing he stumbles over. As he reports this, how do you react to it? In all these situations, are you listening?

That's why people don't understand children. They don't know how to listen to them. (You could write a whole book on that!) People think they can just say to a child, "You behave yourself." And the poor children — all the listening they get is listening to a boss. A good listener isn't bossy.

Do father and mother listen to each other? The children hear what their parents talk about. There would not be so much divorce if people *listened* to one another. Children say, "Nobody listens to me." Listening is an art.

Children feel so wonderful when adults talk things over with them and listen. That's a real education. One of the values of silence is that we learn to listen. But then, real listening is not cheap. Listening costs unhurried time; nearly all people are in a hurry. It requires a forgetfulness of self so that one can see into the heart of another. It requires love and understanding so that one can listen without condemnation. The person who can listen to the heart of another is the one who can open the door to God.

GET BY WITH IT?

What happens when a child needs punishment? When a child knows he's been wrong and you don't do anything about it, the lesson he learns is how to "get by with it." It is a terrible thing for a child to learn that! If he learns that from his parents, then he gets by with all sorts of things. He gets by with getting into the cupboard; he gets by with stealing candy or whatever. The fact that he learns how to "get by" is a terrible lesson, because at sixteen if a fellow is with a girl and hasn't disciplined himself, he'll do anything he wants to at the moment.

If he is not punished when he deserves it — if he learns that this works with his parents — then he thinks he can "get by" with *anything*.

Children get the understanding of what's right and what's wrong from their parents.

Only integrity and consistency in parents can hold the respect of the child. Somehow children seem to have an innate sense of justice. When parents respect the child's integrity, they win the respect of the child. The child seems to learn that together with his parents he and they obey a truth beyond themselves.

FOLLOWING

How do we teach a child to follow? Most children learn something about following when they read the Twenty-third Psalm, "He leadeth me." If you want the little ones to follow you, you have to love them. If you really *love* them, they will want to follow you! Older people with the little ones — but when the little ones follow you, you have to be a good example. Make the example attractive.

I don't know anything more devastating than to be an example for a little fellow. Yes, I mean the word *devastating*, because when you stop to think of it, whenever we ask people to follow us, we take on a real responsibility. Suppose you have a group of three-year-olds and you're going to teach them how to follow. Do you love them so well that they would like to follow whatever you do? We would have no trouble with our teaching if we would do that. The children want to know if we really mean it.

If they *love* you, they will follow you. It will really mean something to them if they have a teacher who

loves them. A teacher has to be so loving and creative that the children *want* to follow him. If they don't follow you, find out why. You'll have no difficulty, if you really love the children. If you have that kind of relationship, there is no danger of being bossy. You won't always have to say, "Behave yourself." They'll *want* to act that way.

There was something so lovely about Jesus and the children. They wanted to run after him and be with him. Jesus was an example as a teacher because he loved every one of the children. They couldn't keep away from him. The main thing is that we *love* the children. Jesus drew the children to him. He loved them. They followed him!

RESPONDING TO LOVE

God has equipped every child with a natural response to love. It must be treasured so that it may grow in capacity for the day when, with all his heart, he begins to respond to the Lord of Life. Jesus always watches for response to the steadily offered love of God. His disciples were slow to learn it, but the *children* he met responded at once!

Although the children of Jesus' day had been taught to stay in the background in the presence of adults, all barriers were broken down when they met Jesus. They flocked to him naturally, gladly. How they must have delighted his heart! Their naturalness in response helped him get his own yearning across to the grownups.

Feeling their adult superiority, his disciples tried to do what so many parents and teachers do: they consciously or unconsciously blocked the natural response of the children to God!

His disciples, of course, acting like most self-important adults, tried to keep the children from "bothering" Jesus. When the Master noticed this, "he was indignant, and said to them, 'Let the children come to me, do not hinder them; for to such belongs the kingdom of God. Truly, I say to you, whoever does not receive the kingdom of God like a child shall not enter it' " (Mark 10:14-15, RSV).

Forgiving

One of the greatest evidences of love is the ability to forgive. We fail in God-love, which is not only giving-love but understanding-love, when we fail to understand a child and why he acts the way he does.

The evidence of this failure toward our children is our tendency to label a child. Labeling a child means to him that he is not forgiven. When a child is labeled, he does not know what to do but to live up to the label!

How can a child understand the forgiveness of God if he never had the experience of forgiveness in his home relationships? The most sacred trust of the home is to train the capacity for love, so that every child can come to know a relationship with God as the Heavenly Father and say in truth, *"Our Father who art in heaven."*

Building Courage

One of the most damaging of careless adult habits is to laugh *at* a child in his presence. One may laugh only *with* a child. We block a child's outreach to life unwittingly, often because we are not conscious of what is happening to and in the child.

It is a great gift to a child to build up his courage so that he can walk always in hope and faith, no matter what happens to him. Those who break a child's spirit must answer to Jesus Christ.

Courage keeps the heart's door open for hope even in the darkness of this world. Hope means that there is a faith that "this is my Father's world." If the child knows that the God of love is the God of his parents, he will never lose his courage, but will find it strengthened and preserved so that he can be set *toward* life and not against it.

GOD LOVE

We misrepresent our Heavenly Father to our children when we lose faith in the power of his love, which he revealed through Jesus, or when we hold in our own hearts a distorted view of this love.

When we turn unwittingly to the methods of the world in forcing our own limited ways and thoughts upon the children, are we afraid that love won't work?

God's heart is broken for the millions who do not know genuine love; this is the reason for the cross.

TO THE YOUNGSTERS

It is wonderful when you find out something you can do!
There are lots of things everyone of us can just do.

- **Obey**

  Obey your father and mother. That's part of the Ten Commandments.
  Obey them, not only because it is right and because you *"ought"* to, but
  because you love them and you *choose* to. What a difference!

- **Listen**

  Doesn't it feel good when grownups take time to listen to you? Be a
  good listener yourself. If you learn to listen to your parents, you will be

ready to listen to God. In fact, God is the Great Listener. He always has time to listen.

- **Choose**

  It's fun to choose. Choose wisely, but be willing to take the consequences when you make a bad choice. That way you'll learn. Sometimes your parents will know the best choice. Then trust them and let them choose for you.

- **Think of others**

  Can you draw a picture? Can you share your toys? If you can't do anything else, *sing*! If you can't sing, then you can say, "Thank you God, thank you for Papa and Mama." And then you can ask, "What can I do for you today?"

- **Love**

  Say, "I love you" to your parents. (They like to be told.) You know they love you and when you "love back," you will learn about *giving* love and

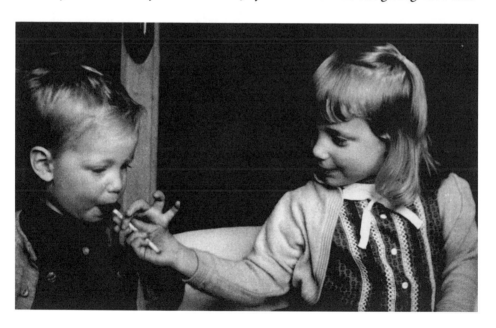

not only *receiving* love. It is not *"I want to be loved,"* but *"I love you."* When you know about *giving* love, you will know about God's love.

Sometimes you don't always feel loving toward everybody. But children, you want to be like Jesus! Jesus loves everybody.

- **Wait**

Learn to wait. Sometimes you want something right now but it may be better to wait. The sooner you learn about patience and waiting for the right time, the happier you'll be.

- **Remember**

God loves all the children. Some of them are black, some are white, some don't speak English. But Jesus loves them all, and we love you.

I tell my children I love them, even when they are naughty. All I want for you is that you love people and don't forget that God loves you.

- **Pray**

You can talk to God. You can thank him. You can tell him when you're sorry. There was once a little five-year-old boy in Roanoke who, after praying one evening, said:

Dear Jesus,
If there is something
I can do for you,
Just let me know.

TO THOSE WHO CARE FOR YOUNGSTERS

Every child comes bringing with him a new chance for a better world, provided you, his parents (and others who care for the child) are awakened to your responsibility.

- **Don't "s-mother" them**

  "S-mother love" is called possessive love. It makes a child very insecure. He has to play all the time to gain favor. "Mother loves you, do this for her" is never a fair premise for a request. A child has not experienced real love unless he learns to love back.

- **Take time**

  When you are especially busy and wish the children would occupy themselves, you gain nothing by pushing them away. But take them up and "hug them good" as if you have nothing to do all day but love them. This assurance from you will set them free to run and play.

- **Enjoy them**

  Don't be caught self-consciously *trying* to love your children. *Enjoy* them! Enjoying children is loving them without anxiety. When there is anxiety, the children seem to pick up the anxiety and miss the attempted love.

- **Respect them**

  It is easy in our busy lives to forget the child has feelings and to respect them. He has a hard time knowing how important he is to God if his parents do not have the same respect for him.

- **Don't be irritated**

  When we let ourselves be irritated by children, this irritation reveals more about ourselves than about the child. Such irritations come because of love failure within ourselves and not from without by some act of the child, however disobedient he may seem.

- **Don't make the child the center of attention**

  Anything that fastens a child's attention upon himself so that he wants to be the *center of attention* is no help to proper self-development. There is nothing in which otherwise good parents fail more regularly than in talking about the children in their presence.

- **Treat a child as a person**

  Children want to be people, not things to be discussed like new furniture. It can be just as damaging to "explain" a child in his hearing as to punish him before other people. It cannot be said too often that talking about a child in his presence makes him a *thing* and not a person. He wants to be a person in his own right. Children light up with a new outreaching life when treated as people, but they soak up thoughtless comments, abuse, and unkindness like a sponge, and doors to life close in on them.

- **Let them play**

  Play is much more than something to keep the children busy while their parents are otherwise occupied. Play is the school room where the children learn life values.

  The "make-believe" world of a little child is his real world. For a preschool child, *play* is his *work*, his whole life. (Adults forget this sometimes because play for them is release from work.)

  The ingenuity of a child's imagination at play usually exceeds that of an adult. Play is the child's means of discovery of communication and of expression.

- **Share their joy in nature**

  Children seem especially sensitive to the appeal of beauty. The lovely things of nature stir them easily to wonder. This inborn sense of wonder is quickly turned to reverence and worship. Share it with them.

- **Let him do it "by myself"**

  A child has a real growing joy in doing whatever he is able to do "all by my lone." No wise adult will do for a child what he can do for himself. (If he does, the child will soon give up and let the adult do it!)

  But the child needs boundaries. His parent-set boundaries need to be out far enough for him to have freedom for experimentation, but not too far beyond his responsible learning.

• Help them think of others

As a child learns to think of others, he will grow out of doing things to draw attention to himself. He will learn to have security within himself so he does not feel the need to lash out at others or to manipulate them in order to feel that he is a human being with dignity.

A child is possessive of his toys as he learns the responsibility of ownership, but he has to learn to share with others.

As he learns to think of others' needs, he will not mind so much the limits he must face for himself.

• Prepare

Prepare children for what God can do for and with them. The importance of this preparation cannot be exaggerated. The how and when it happens that God comes to us is his gift. The preparation, the opening the door, the being ready is our responsibility.

• Open the door

God comes to anyone, anywhere, at any age, whenever a door is open for his coming. He does not ask us our age or to fill out a questionnaire about our theological background or lack of it. He lets us come just as we are (with our confessions of sin and self-centeredness). All he asks is that we come with a whole heart, ready to learn from him.

ANNA'S PRAYER

We failed you in many ways;
now we come in complete confidence.
We want only your Word.
That comes from
the bottom of our hearts.
It's hard for us to understand
how we could even question
what your Word might be.
We know that in
the days that are clouded
you are with us
in full love!
We have one faith
and that is your way.
It is by far the best way.
And we want to be your children
without question.
It looks silly
from a human standpoint
in our situation.
But we come with all the things
that are hard for us.
We praise you because we can trust you.
We can do the things you want
because you give us strength.
We don't have to do it in our own strength.
Thank you,
because we can trust you.
Thank you,
because we can have complete confidence
in you.

*This — Anna's last spoken prayer — was said in a clear voice after a difficult
morning of impaired speech on May 13, 1985.*

ABOUT THE AUTHOR

Anna Beahm Mow was born in Daleville, Virginia, on July 31, 1893, the daughter of Mary and I.N.H. Beahm and the sister of Sara, William, Esther, Mary, and Lois. Both her parents were educators and provided a stimulating childhood. When her mother's health failed, Anna, the oldest, had a large responsibility in caring for the family. Her love of cooking and sewing began early. Her father, Isaac Newton Harvey, a colorful preacher in the Church of the Brethren (affectionately called "Brother Beahm"), was president of two colleges he helped to establish. He was vigorous and lively until he died at the age of ninety-one in an automobile accident on his way to a preaching engagement.

In 1914, after graduating from one of the high schools her father established, Anna left home to study at Bethany Bible School in Chicago and later at Manchester College. Because she wished to go to India as a missionary, she returned to Bethany to prepare further for this. She became a close friend of a fellow student, Anetta Mow, whose brother Baxter, a Rhodes Scholar, was studying at Oxford University in England. He later taught Hebrew and studied at Bethany Seminary where he met Anna and shared her longing to go to India. They were married on Baxter's birthday, March 30, 1921.

Following graduation, their first assignment was to home missions in the Blue Ridge Mountains of Virginia. Their first home was a log house, "one room and a path," among simple mountain folk they grew to love.

India became reality in 1923 where they won the hearts of the Indian people through "serving those who were in no position to help themselves." Baxter and Anna returned to America in 1940 with their three children, Lois, Joe, and Merrill, all born in India. They did not return to India as planned since Anna was asked to teach at Bethany.

They "retired" in 1958 and moved to Roanoke, Virginia, but the message of their lives and convictions had already touched so many that retirement was not really what took place. Anna continued to travel widely, teaching and lecturing and visiting her grandchildren. She wrote ten books and was determined to write another when she suffered a disabling stroke in January 1985.

Anna had become a very firm and close friend of the Bruderhof, and after her stroke she moved to the New Meadow Run Bruderhof in Farmington, Pennsylvania. There she spent the last five months of her life with her son Merrill and his family and those she loved. She was nearly 92 when she died on July 7 at New Meadow Run Bruderhof, now also the place of her burial.

————————

Anyone whose life has ever touched hers knows of her delicious humor. Yet, for her, tears of understanding come as easily as that laugh. She has shown me again and again how thin is the line that separates sorrow from joy – God's kind of joy, God's kind of sorrow. She was devoid of burdensome self-consciousness and in a naturalness before God was "simply eager for everything God had up ahead for her."

—quotes from Dottie Murray in Sister Anna

The brightness and joy, the humor and depth of insight, and perhaps above all the sensitivity to the presence and working of the Spirit - all these we feel as we think of her. It helps us realize that these must be among the characteristics of Eternity.

—Art Wiser, July 7, 1985

Her circle of love was small enough to minister to those close at hand, but large enough to include prime ministers and kings, princes and prelates. She was at home with all.

She could be a good neighbor with those who lived next door, but she moved easily in many places of a world neighborhood.

She was equally at ease in the pulpit as she was in a kitchen; in a classroom as by a campfire; with large audiences as in a private conversation. She could relate to women and men, to children and older people. She knew nothing about generation gaps or gender gaps or social, racial, or faith dividing lines.

She practiced what she preached and knew well what St. Francis once told a student of his: "There is little value in going anywhere to preach the gospel unless we preach the gospel everywhere we go."

—from Anna's memorial service in
Roanoke, July 25, 1985

In her forthright way, she was able to represent such a childlike trust, with courage and "salt." She had no use for milk-and-water discipleship and could always say a straight word that could puncture anyone's self-esteem. Yet the way in which she cared so deeply about each one showed that she did it for love of Jesus. Her fiery love for Jesus and reliance on God, whatever she had to go through, has been a witness for Him and in this we rejoice and will always remember her.

—J. A. Bush, New York

My years as her editor made me consider her a dear and valued friend. Anna was one of the most Godly people I have been privileged to know, yet her wisdom and knowledge of the world, its literature and its leaders, never ceased to amaze me – along with her cookbook collection! I was honored to have known her and will miss her cheery notes.

—Judith Markham, Zondervan,
Grand Rapids, Michigan

I laughed, got teary-eyed, learned, and was stimulated when I read the manuscript *Two or Ninety-Two.* One line of hers really struck me: "The pesky thing is, I can still think." Even at her advanced age and physical deterioration, she *could* and did still think.

I did not know her as "Grandma," but to so many thousands, myself included, she was a human, wise, witty, steadfast friend. Her thoughts and wisdom during her final five months would make the perfect gift book for persons in nursing homes – or just old and wondering.

—Eugenia Price

READERS RESPOND

I did enjoy touching base with Anna's thoughts again. I can see the book to be of interest and value to more than the family, both because she was a woman of wisdom and because many knew her. —*Helen Alderfer*

I read it with great pleasure, joy and stimulation! —*Dottie Murray*

It is special to have in hand those gems from Anna Mow — for any time, I'm inclined. Her witness lives on in everyone who knew her — and now for those who didn't have that chance. —*Pep Hinkey*

I am so glad for what Anna Mow has written. Her life and writings bring a light from Christ into our dark world. —*Maureen Burn*

We really enjoyed reading our mother Mow's book, it's so down to earth and full of warmth and love. —*R & L Keiderling*

I spent a few happy hours going over *Two or Ninety-Two*. Heartwarming and tender influences come from the pages. —*Art and Mary Wiser*

I am so glad to have a copy to enjoy and share. Your Mother Anna was such a down-to-earth, no-nonsense person, and we can learn a lot from her in many ways. —*Barbara Greenyer*

We enjoyed reading it very much. It was almost like sitting down and talking with her. While we miss her very much, we feel her presence with us and recall with such pleasure our years of ministry together at Bethany. —*Paul Robinson*

The book is most heartwarming. Those of us who knew her can almost hear her saying some of the words in the book, and hear her delightful chuckle. —*Kay Alwine*

We remember Anna very well from her visits to Woodcrest. Now we are nearing ninety and need the kind of spirit she had, which you have captured in this little book. We'll keep it handy to turn to when we start feeling sorry for ourselves. —*Tom and Florrie Potts*

ACKNOWLEDGMENTS

Anna's daughter Lois, her son Joe, and Merrill's wife, Kathy, and their families wish to thank all who helped this book become a reality. We are grateful to Merrill who edited and put together the manuscript from typed notes. But before it was completed one year after his mother's death, he was diagnosed with cancer. He met this blow of sickness and faced death in the same childlike faith as his mother. It was his wish that his mother's witness of hope and courage and complete trust in God be shared with others.

...to the Bruderhof who made it possible for our mother, Anna, to spend her last months among her family and brothers and sisters in New Meadow Run.

...to our doctor and nurses and brothers and sisters who stood by with their love and encouragement.

...to the children who visited and were a source of joy and delight with their songs and artwork.

...to the young people whom she especially loved and who came to her to share their concerns.

...to many sisters who helped our family with her care and filled notebooks full for this book. And to those who typed up the notes, read the manuscript, and helped it all come together.

Part I contains quotations either direct or paraphrased from Anna's book *So Who's Afraid of Birthdays*. Quotations from *Preparing Your Child to Love God* are in Part II. Photos from the family albums are mostly of Anna, Baxter, their children, grandchildren, and great-grandchildren.

Page 18: Anna with Rosa Page Welch

Page 22: Anna's mother, Mary Bucher Beahm

Page 30: Anna with Hans and Margrit Meier, Deer Spring Bruderhof

Page 31: Anna in England at the Darvell Bruderhof with Sara Maendel, Margrit Meier, Dorothy Barron, Phyllis Woolston, Kathleen Hasenberg.

Page 33: Anna with fellow India missionaries Charlotte Wiser and Nanna Moody, who were visiting their sons at the Woodcrest Bruderhof.